P9-CQA-862

Christian Etienne
French Master Chef

Wonderful *Provençal* cuisine

Photographs
Didier Benaouda

Editions OUEST-FRANCE

Contents

Good, high-class cuisine is steeped in character, a local accent and a sense of friendship. Christian Etienne has plenty of character, a pronounced accent and, as far as friendship is concerned, there is plenty to share! His character comes from Provence, his accent is Provençal, and his friendship is both proverbial and Mediterranean.

Provence is an austere but highly-scented region, a region that is unforgettable. When Christian worked at the Intercontinental, he was on the staff with Gagnaire (if you please!). They talked about lambs, the herbs growing on the hillsides, red mullet and dace, olive oil, tender young vegetables and other light, mouthwatering, sun-soaked products that are only to be found south of Montélimar.

Christian retained his nostalgia amid the rush and bustle of the great hotel and he learned a lot! Anybody with in-bred skill always finds something to learn. Then Christian returned home, to the region of his birth, an area full of tomatoes and truffles, warmed by the sun, swept by the great mistral wind that clears the air, the mind and the heart. Christian came home, determined to pay homage to the land of Provence and the women who gave him his vocation – his two grandmothers and his mother who delighted the family with everything that the gardens and orchards had to offer, backed up by plenty of family love.

Christian has brought two additional touches to this typical Provençal cuisine – the skills of top-class cuisine as practised by one of the finalists in the competition to find the Best Chef in France – and his own personal touch, his touch of class!

In this book, he guides you through Provençal cuisine with its stuffed vegetables, braised dishes and some outstanding culinary experiences. He does so in a kindly, discreet manner for true men of Provence are both kind and retiring.

You will find out exactly what makes a good ratatouille and a subtle fisherman's pie. You will discover how ordinary chick peas can be raised to sublime heights by olive oil. You will learn how to make fennel sorbet and pine-kernel tart. When you serve stuffed Provençal mullet to your friends, you will be wearing a chef's hat, handed down by a great chef famous for his kindness and friendliness... Gradually you too will acquire the accent, discover the Camargue and scrub, learn about Provence through the subtlest of its features – its flavours and its aromas!

So it's off to the stove, stew pans and cooking pots and – bon appétit!

Robert Ledrole

Hors d'œuvres

Herb and Tomato Tartar
with raw shallot

Serves 6

10 large tomatoes • 1 shallot • 1 bunch of basil
olive oil from Maussane • salt, pepper

- Skin tomatoes, slice, remove seeds and roughly chop flesh.
- Press for as long as possible.
- Moisten with olive oil.
- Season with salt and pepper. Add chopped basil and sliced shallot.
- Place in round moulds to serve, dribbling olive oil over at the last minute.

Snail and Mild Garlic Soup

Serves 4

1 litre tomato puree • 200 g tomatoes (flesh only)
100 g cloves garlic (peeled) • 100 g flat parsley
24 or 48 tinned snails (quantity depends on personal preference) • milk • salt, pepper

• If the garlic is old, remove sprouts and use 120 g.

• Heat puree.

• Blanch garlic three times to remove all trace of bitterness. To do so, place cloves in a small saucepan, cover with cold milk and bring to boil. Remove from heat as soon as milk boils, drain garlic and throw away milk. Repeat this procedure twice more.

• Drain snails. If you are using wild snails, leave to disgorge then cook with a few cloves garlic and a large sprig of fennel. Drain.

• Heat snails in a frying pan with olive oil and add finely chopped garlic, stirring it in gently. Season with salt and pepper.

• Roughly cut up parsley and sprinkle over snails. Stir once or twice. Place mixture in a verrine.

• Add tomato flesh to boiling puree. Then pour into the soup verrines and stir carefully before serving.

Pressed Mackerel
and fennel

Serves 10

2 kg mackerel • 2 kg fennel • 50 cl white wine • 2 carrots
2 onions • 4 cloves garlic • 1 g saffron • thyme, bay leaf, olive oil

• Fillet mackerel. Season with salt and pepper and lay out flat on a baking tray. Oil lightly.

• Bring white wine to the boil and pour over fillets. Boil fillets for 2 to 3 seconds only. Set aside and leave to cool.

• Meanwhile, cut fennel into six pieces. Blanch in salted water (boil for 4 minutes and always use 14 g salt to 1 litre water). Cool and drain.

• Finely chop carrots and onions. In a pan big enough to take the fennel, fry onions and carrots until almost ready to colour.

• Add chopped garlic and place fennel over the top. Add saffron, salt and pepper. Pour on white wine used to cook the mackerel and finish off with water so that the fennel is well covered. Cook over a low heat.

• When fennel is cooked, remove from pan and drain.

• Reduce remaining liquor by half. Prepare a terrine, alternating layers of mackerel and fennel. Blend in remaining liquor and put in a cold place overnight.

• The next day, slice using an electric knife and serve cold with a fines herbes vinaigrette.

This recipe goes very well with a white Côtes-du-Rhône wine (Domaine de la Présidente).

Mixed Asparagus Salad

Serves 10

30 green asparagus tips • 30 white asparagus tips
20 g chopped black olives • preserved tomatoes
Vinaigrette: 1 tbsp balsamic vinegar
6 tbsp olive oil • salt, pepper • 15 g chopped chives
2 g chopped tarragon • 5 g chopped flat parsley • 10 g preserved tomatoes
enough mixed green salad for all the guests

• Place mixed green salad in the centre of the plate. Lay the white and green asparagus tips alternately on top of the lettuce to form a dome.

• Sprinkle with preserved tomatoes and black olives and moisten with vinaigrette.

Asparagus is the most outstanding of all spring vegetables. It reaches our tables just after the end of winter, the period during which we eat a lot of game and pork products. In days gone by, people used to say that, with its marked diuretic properties, asparagus arrived to purify the body.

Whether white, purple or green, this is a very tasty vegetable. The larger the asparagus, the more the taste, but it always has to be eaten very fresh.

Sardine and Tomato Quiche

SERVES 6

1 CAKE TIN, DIA. 30 CM (12 IN.) • 300 G HOME-PRESERVED TOMATOES
500 G FRESH SARDINES • THYME • OLIVE OIL, SALT, PEPPER • 300 G PUFF PASTRY

• Line the tin with puff pastry. Bake blind, covering pastry base with dried haricot beans or butter beans to prevent it from rising. Bake through, until golden.

• Meanwhile, fillet sardines. Drain well on a cloth.

• When pastry base is cooked, leave to cool then spread preserved tomatoes over base. Lay out sardines to form a wheel, tails towards the centre.

• Season with salt and pepper, sprinkle with thyme, dribble on olive oil and bake in a hot oven (170 to 180 °C) for 10 minutes.

Preserved tomatoes

• Choose long Italian tomatoes for this recipe. They should be red and ripe but not over-ripe. Cut in half, remove seeds and lay out on a baking sheet leaving plenty of space between them.

• Season with salt and pepper, sprinkle on a pinch of sugar, dust with thyme to flavour and add additional flavour with a few cloves of garlic (crushed).

• Pour on some olive oil and leave in the oven for 4 hours at 100 °C.

• Put in a cool place for a few days.

Lamb Dumplings

Serves 10

500 g well-braised pieces of neck, loin or breast • 200 g cooked spinach
50 g cooked sorrel • 100 g onions (finely chopped and cooked)
150 to 200 g pork caul • 5 juniper berries
thyme, bay leaf, sage • 1 litre stock

• Cut lamb into small pieces and cook slowly as if making a stew. This produces a good, dry dumpling.

• Make dumpling with spinach, onion, garlic, thyme and game and crushed juniper berries.

• Make small balls weighing approximately 30 g (just over 1 oz.) and roll in caul.

• Lay out in an ovenproof dish and pour on stock, half covering the dumplings.

• Place sage and bay leaves on top and cook for a good hour at a low heat (140 °C).

Pork Cheese
with fines herbes

1/2 head of a pig, with tongue • 1 knuckle • 2 trotters • 3 carrots
2 onions stuck with 5 cloves • 2 sticks green celery
1 whole garlic (halved) • thyme, bay leaf • 40 g parsley
30 g chives • 15 g tarragon

• Clean head, trotters, knuckle and tongue by soaking for half-a-day in fresh water. Clean head and trotters well and cut or burn off any remaining bristles.

• When all ingredients are clean, place in a large pan. Cover with water, stir well, add salt (14 g cooking salt to 1 litre water) and pepper (3 g pepper for 1 l water). Cook for 5 hours, skimming regularly to remove any impurities rising to the surface.

• At the end of the 5 hours, allow to cool until the pieces of meat can be removed. Remove all bones and roughly chop meat. Place in a terrine that is big enough to leave room to mix the ingredients. Check seasoning and add fines herbes.

• Fill several terrines or jars with chopped meat and add cooking liquor at the last moment. Mix well to ensure that the stock soaks into all the meat.

• Place terrines in a cold place and leave for 2 or 3 days before eating with a crusty farmhouse loaf and a good glass of red wine e.g. Château La Nerthe (Châteauneuf-du-Pape).

Fisherman's Pie
with garlic croutons

1 kg salt cod • 1 kg cod • 1 litre milk • 1 litre olive oil
1 whole garlic • 1 baguette

- On the previous day, soak cod to remove salt. Poach with fresh cod in milk then thicken with olive oil. Drain.
- Using a wooden spoon or spatula, stir vigorously over a very low heat and blend in olive oil until smooth.
- At the last minute, blend in crushed, pureed garlic. Check seasoning (be careful not to add too much salt).
- Spread on toasted slices of baguette.

"Brandade" is one of the greatest specialities of the town of Nîmes. In days gone by, the people of Nîmes used to trade with fishermen, exchanging fish for salt. They removed the salt from the cod by placing it in the cistern over the toilet.

White Wine and Rabbit Terrine

SERVES 10

1 home-bred rabbit • 2 carrots • 5 shallots • 1 onion • 3 cloves garlic
2 oranges (zests only) • 1 lemon (zest only) • 1.5 litres white Châteauneuf-du-Pape wine
salt, pepper • 20 g chopped flat parsley • 20 g chopped chives
10 g tarragon • thyme, bay leaf

• Bone rabbit and cut into large pieces.

• Roughly chop carrots, shallot, onion and garlic.

• Finely dice orange and lemon zests.

• Mix all dry ingredients and pour on Châteauneuf-du-Pape. Marinate for 24 hours.

• To make stock with bones: sweat bones in a large saucepan, then cover with water and add thyme and bay leaf. Simmer very gently until almost reduced away.

• The next day, add fines herbes and stock to marinated rabbit. Season with 14 g salt per kilo and 3 g pepper. Place mixture in a terrine and cook for 3 hours in a moderate oven (140 to 160 °C).

• Once cooked, leave to cool. Do not serve until the following day.

It is delightful served with a few gherkins and pickled onions. It is also very tasty with a few lettuce leaves or peppers marinated in olive oil.

Small, Tarragon-stuffed Tomatoes

Serves 6

18 small round tomatoes • 2 kg marmande tomatoes • 10 tarragon leaves
25 cl beef stock • 2 cloves garlic • 1 onion • olive oil

• Skin small tomatoes and remove seeds. Place upside down to drain.

• Take 2 kg Marmande tomatoes: skin, remove seeds, dice.

• Sweat onion and garlic in olive oil with diced tomatoes.

• Reduce down.

• Add chopped tarragon leaves and fill tomatoes.

• Cook for 10 minutes in a hot oven with beef stock and serve as they are.

This is a mouthwatering accompaniment to red meats or oily fish such as mackerel or sardines. On their own, the tomatoes can be eaten hot or cold.

Lamb's Brain
with capers

1 or 2 lamb's brains • 1 bay leaf • flour • butter
olive oil • 30 g capers

If serving as an hors d'œuvre, allow one brain for two; for a main dish, allow one brain per person.

• Clean for a few hours in fresh water to remove any traces of blood. Poach in salted water containing vinegar and a bay leaf. Bring to boil and leave in water to cool.

• Drain the brain, cut into quarters, dust with flour and fry in a hot pan containing a mixture of one-half butter and one-half olive oil. Fry until golden on all sides and place on a serving dish.

• Remove any fat remaining in frying pan and add lightly chopped capers. Add 50 g butter and fry until golden brown.

• Pour over brains, which should be eaten very hot accompanied by a few lettuce leaves and a light red wine.

Poultry Liver Flan

Serves 6 to 8

200 g poultry livers • 6 eggs • 1 litre single cream
salt, pepper, nutmeg • 2 grey shallots • 1 clove garlic

• Liquidise ingredients. Be careful not to overheat and introduce too much air into livers. Turn liquidiser on and off in short bursts. Season with 10 g salt, 3 g pepper, and some grated nutmeg. Pass through a fine-meshed Chinese sieve. The mixture should be moist.

• Lightly grease dariole moulds. Fill with mixture and cook in a bain-marie at 180° C for 2 hours.

• Cool and store for 3 days in the refrigerator. It takes 3 days to bring out and blend the flavours.

Fish

Roast Cod

Serves 4

1 piece cod (600 g) • 4 tomatoes • garlic • parsley • sea salt
olive oil • balsamic vinegar • salt, pepper • flour

• Rub piece of cod with sea salt and leave for 1 hour in a clean teatowel.

• Meanwhile, slice tomatoes fairly thickly. Dust with flour and fry in olive oil until golden. Remove immediately from pan and drain on kitchen paper.

• Finely chop garlic and parsley.

• Preheat oven (180 °C).

• Carefully wash cod under cold water. Drain and dry then cut into four fillets. Lay fillets in a dish and pour on olive oil.

• Roast fish in the oven, with skin uppermost, for 8 to 10 minutes.

• Arrange sliced tomato on a serving dish.

• As soon as fish is cooked, switch off oven and put tomatoes in oven to keep warm. Remove skin from cod and lay fish out over sliced tomatoes.

• Recover cooking liquor from fish, add a few drops balsamic vinegar, chopped parsley and garlic. Serve the sauce with the fish.

Red Mullet
with fried Italian tomatoes

Serves 6

6 red mullet • 6 Italian tomatoes (ripe but firm) • 3 shallots
12 black olives • balsamic vinegar, olive oil
a few sprigs dill

• Prepare mullet fillets, removing bones with tweezers.

• Skin tomatoes. Cut lengthways, remove seeds and season with salt. Drain.

• Meanwhile, finely chop shallots. Stone olives and chop roughly with a knife.

• Prepare a vinaigrette with olive oil, balsamic vinegar, salt and pepper.

• Fry tomatoes with olive oil. Add shallots. Leave to rest then lay out on plates.

• Fry red mullets skin side down then turn over and fry on fleshy side. Do not overcook. Lay on tomatoes.

• Decorate with sprigs of dill and chopped black olives. Pour on vinaigrette.

• Dress the fish on hot plates with the garnish.

• Drizzle with olive oil just before serving.

Grilled Tuna Fish
with mixed pepper cones

Serves 6

6 tuna steaks • 1 red pepper • 1 yellow pepper
1 green pepper • 1 large onion (finely chopped) • 1 clove garlic
balsamic vinegar and olive oil • 2 gelatin sheets

- Finely dice peppers and blanch in salted water. Cool immediately in iced water.
- Sweat onions in olive oil, add peppers and crushed garlic. Brown slightly. Place in blender, blend and add gelatin sheets while still hot. Mix well and fill cone-shaped moulds.
- Grill tuna steaks, being careful not to overcook as tuna can rapidly become dry. Lay steaks on peppers.
- Pour on vinaigrette.

Enjoy this dish with a good Tavel produced by the Roudil family.

Ask your fishmonger to give you some good steaks 3 to 4 cm (1 or 2 inches) thick weighing 130 to 150 g each depending on your appetite.

Oyster Soup

Serves 6

18 Bouzigues or vertes de claire oysters • 80 g butter • 100 g flour
1 litre well-flavoured chicken stock • 1/2 lemon (juice only) • salt, pepper

• Open oysters, strain juice and set aside.

• Make a cream sauce. Prepare a roux by melting butter, adding flour and stirring briefly. To ensure that roux stays white, avoid overcooking flour on an excessively high heat. Cool roux then pour on stock; this method avoids the formation of lumps.

• Whip, place back on the heat for 30 minutes. Strain then check consistency, adding stock or reducing down again. The soup should resemble single cream.

• Do not add salt. Season with pepper and nutmeg.

• Add juice from oysters and put back on heat with lemon juice.

• Lay oysters out in each plate then pour on boiling soup which will seal in their flavour without overcooking.

Mushroom-stuffed Calamaries

Serves 4 to 6

200 to 300 g calamaries • 500 g penny bun mushrooms • 20 g dried penny bun mushrooms
500 g button mushrooms • 1 young penny bun mushroom per person
3 shallots (finely chopped) • 2 cloves garlic • 10 g fresh parsley (chopped) • olive oil

• Dice penny bun mushrooms and fry in oil seasoned with salt and pepper. Drain in a colander or sieve.

• Finely chop button mushrooms. Sauté shallots with a small quantity of olive oil. When shallots are golden, add button mushrooms and cook until liquor has reduced away. Leave to cool then mix penny buns, button mushrooms, dried penny bun mushrooms, finely chopped garlic and parsley.

• Check seasoning to ensure that the stuffing is to your taste.

• Clean calamaries. Pull head away to gut and remove legs and rinse well in cold water. Drain and dry slightly on an electric ring.

• Cut legs at eye level (eyes are discarded). Fry and blend into stuffing.

• Fill calamaries using an icing bag and close with a toothpick. Fry in a hot frying pan until golden on each side. Complete cooking by baking for a few minutes in the oven.

• Wash and fry the young penny bun mushrooms in butter.

Calamaries can be served as they are with a side salad and good herb vinaigrette or with a crab coulis and a little grated parmesan cheese.

Lobster
with orange butter and Chinese anise

Serves 2

2 lobster (600 to 650 g) • 4 oranges • 2 g ground chinese anise • 300 g butter
2 courgettes • 1 carrot • 8 small spring onions

• Bring salted water containing vinegar to the boil in a large saucepan. When boiling, place lobsters in pan. N.B. The lobsters must be alive. Cover pan to avoid splashes. Cook for no more than 2 minutes after water has returned to the boil. Remove lobster from water and leave to cool on a baking tray.

• Meanwhile, squeeze oranges and strain juice through a fine-meshed sieve. Reduce down until juice resembles a fairly liquid syrup then blend in butter as if making a white butter sauce. Add Chinese anise and set aside.

• Cut strips of courgettes and carrots. Cook for a few minutes in salted water but be careful – they cook very quickly. Cool in iced water to ensure that courgettes remain green.

• Remove lobster from shell, including tail and pincers. Keep carcasses to make something else (e.g. lobster coulis or American Sauce). Cut tail in two lengthways.

• Fry everything in olive oil. Lobster should be slightly browned to improve its taste.

• Lay lobster on plates, arrange vegetables on top or round about and pour on orange butter.

Bouillabaisse

Fish soup: 3 kg red soup • 1 leek • 1 head fennel
3 whole garlic (halved) • 1 onion • 250 g tomato puree
2 g saffron • thyme, bay leaf

• Sweat all vegetables without allowing to colour. Add fish (red soup), tomato puree and saffron. Stir well until fish falls to pieces. Cover with water and cook for 3 hours at a slow rolling boil.

• Strain through a Chinese sieve (not too fine mesh). Correct seasoning (salt, pepper) then keep hot. There should be at least 5 litres stock left.

fish: 5 medium-sized mullet (200 g per fish)
2 John Dory fillets (500 g per fillet), cut into 10 portions • 5 weevers (100 g per weever)
1 small conger eel (cut into slices of approx. 80 g each)
5 medium-sized scorpion fish (200 g each) • 5 red gurnard (200 g each)

• Take three wide-necked sauté pans. In one, place red gurnard and weevers; in another, scorpion fish and mullet; in the third conger eel and John Dory. Pour over olive oil and sprinkle with fine sea salt.

• Then pour in enough soup to barely cover fish and begin to cook. Once fish is cooked, keep hot.

Royal Bream
with tomatoes and fennel

SERVES 6

1 ROYAL BREAM (1 TO 1.2 KG) • 150 G PRESERVED TOMATOES
1 KG UNCOOKED TOMATOES (MARMANDE TYPE) • 25 CL GOOD WHITE WINE • 2 FENNEL
SALT, PEPPER • NUTMEG, CORIANDER SEEDS • OLIVE OIL

• Prepare, gut, and rinse bream. Remove scales. Lay fish flat on a board. Slash deeply along back fin towards backbone. This facilitates cooking and ensures that fish cooks regularly. Rub salt into slash and stuff fish with preserved tomatoes.

• Preheat oven (160 °C).

• Prepare and quarter fennel.

• Cook in lightly salted water, turning off heat before fennel is completely cooked (the fennel is "blanched" to ensure that it then cooks correctly with tomatoes).

• Slice tomatoes and lay in an ovenproof dish. Finely chop fennel and scatter over tomatoes then top with stuffed bream.

• Pour on white wine, olive oil, grated nutmeg and coriander seeds.

• Season with salt and pepper and cook for 20 minutes.

• Remove and set aside fish. Reduce garnish to a rough puree of fennel and tomatoes.

Dace Steaks
with ratatouille and black olives

Serves 6

1 large sea dace (2 to 3 kg) • olive oil
ratatouille (see recipe under vegetables) • a few black olives

- Debone the sea dace by making a slit along its belly or, as it is a fairly difficult job, ask the fishmonger to do it for you, making sure you keep the bones.
- Place the fish on an oiled baking sheet.
- Fill with ratatouille to the equivalent weight in bones.
- Roll it until it resumes its original shape.
- Poach for 15 minutes then set aside.
- Leave the fish to stand for 10 minutes in its stock.
- Heat the ratatouille after adding black olives. Serve piping hot.

Sea dace is without doubt one of the most highly-prized fish in the south of France.

It can reach a weight of 7 or 8 kg or more, although I have not seen a larger one for a long time. In my opinion, the best weight is 3 kg if you want to serve several people. However, smaller dace are also very tasty and, for two people, 800 g to 1 kg is sufficient.

John Dory
Wellington

Serves 6

6 fillets of John Dory (remove skin first)
2 potatoes (use a good mashing variety) • 1 shallot (finely chopped) • 1 glass white wine
300 g butter • 20 g diced preserved lemon • 1 piece ginger

• Slice potatoes very thinly as if making crisps.

• Do not wash potatoes; it is the starch in them which ensures that they cling to the fish.

• Grate ginger over John Dory and rub in (do not use too much; there should be just enough ginger to add flavour).

• Lay potatoes over fillets like fish scales.

• Heat oil and a small knob of butter in a frying pan.

• Begin frying fillets with potato side downwards.

• Once potatoes are golden brown, carefully turn fillets over and complete cooking, over a low heat.

• Meanwhile, reduce white wine with shallots and beat in butter as if making a white butter sauce.

• Correct seasoning. Add diced preserved lemon just before serving.

• Serve fillets with potato side uppermost and pour butter round about.

Mussel and Saffron Soup

Serves 10

4 kg mussels • 50 cl white wine • 2 carrots (finely chopped)
1 onion (finely chopped) • 2 cloves garlic (finely chopped) • 1 tomato
1 g saffron • pepper, thyme, bay leaf, olive oil

• Wash mussels well. Steam open in white wine with thyme and bay leaf but do not overcook or mussels will be rubbery and dry.

• Remove from shells and set aside in a soup tureen.

• Strain cooking liquor ensuring that there is no sand left (it often drops to the bottom of the saucepan).

• Heat olive oil in another pan, add carrots and onions. When golden, add garlic then tomato and saffron.

• Taste mussel cooking liquor to ensure that it is not too salty before pouring over vegetables. If it is too salty, add water.

• Bring to boil and pour very hot liquor over mussels.

• Serve with grilled croutons rubbed with garlic or with rouille.

We often use mussels from the Etang de Tau but the soup can also be made with mussels grown on stakes, which are smaller but sometimes fuller.

Sole with Asparagus

Serves 6

12 fillets of sole (60 to 80 g each) • 36 green asparagus (well peeled)
2 shallots • 25 cl dry white wine • 300 g butter
20 g fines herbes (parsley, tarragon, chervil) • 1 lemon (juice only)

• Cook asparagus in well salted water and cool immediately in cold salted water.

• Cut asparagus tips slightly longer than the width of the fillets of sole.

• Wrap fillets of sole around asparagus tips.

• Stand in a sauté pan, on finely chopped shallots, with green asparagus tip uppermost.

• Pour in white wine and cook for 10 to 15 minutes over a low heat, with a lid on.

• Meanwhile, dice remainder of asparagus.

• Once sole is cooked, remove from pan and reduce cooking liquor by three-quarters. Whisk in butter.

• At the last moment, add diced asparagus, chopped herbs and lemon juice.

• Reheat all ingredients and lay sole on a serving dish with piping hot braised asparagus round about.

Sole is a fish with an excellent flavour. Nobody ever tires of sole and there are a thousand and one ways of preparing it. Cook it whole if small, or in fillets for larger fish.

Served "à la meunière" or poached, it is an easy fish to work with and is full of taste.

Breaded Roast Fish
with garlic mayonnaise

Serves 2

several small monkfish tails • 300 g breadcrumbs
20 g thyme • olive oil • 6 cloves garlic • 2 eggs
100 g butter • lemon juice • sea salt

- Skin and trim the monkfish tails, stick with a few cloves garlic and cover in breadcrumbs mixed with thyme.
- Bake in a low oven with olive oil and butter (180 °C), basting often with cooking liquor.
- Crush garlic and a small pinch sea salt with a pestle and mortar. When crushed garlic is smooth, add egg yolks and gradually blend in olive oil to produce required quantity.
- Remove monkfish from oven and place on a serving dish. The garlic mayonnaise should be served in a sauce boat.

Meat dishes

Roast Partridge
with cabbage chartreuse

Serves 4

2 partridge • 1 savoy cabbage • 2 onions (chopped) • 2 carrots (chopped)
100 g diced gammon • 5 cloves garlic

• Quarter cabbage. Remove stalks from middle and set aside green leaves. Braise white leaves with chopped onions and carrots, and gammon which has previously sweated. Bake for 2 hours in an oven at 130 to 150 °C.

• Roast partridge with cloves of garlic for 5 minutes on each wing and 5 minutes on the back. Leave partridge to rest for at least 10 minutes. Bone and set aside breast fillets in the fatty liquor produced by the bird during cooking. If legs are still pink, wrap in greaseproof paper to finish cooking.

• Break up carcass and make some good-flavoured stock by just covering with water and cooking until liquor has reduced by half. Strain liquor through a Chinese sieve and set aside.

• Meanwhile, use a 5 cm (2 inch) mould 3 to 4 cm (1 1/4 to 1 3/4 inches) in height to make a cabbage chartreuse. Line with green cabbage leaves. Braise and recook in a hot oven (150 to 160 °C) for 30 minutes.

• Lay the partridge breasts in a serving dish or on individual plates with legs on the side and piping hot gravy round about.

• Serve with a good Châteauneuf-du-Pape or a red Gigondas.

Crown of Pork
with choriso

Serves 8

1 crown pork (6 chops) • 200 g slices of strong choriso (spicy sausage) • 1 onion
1 carrot • 6 cloves garlic • thyme, bay leaf, sprig of sage

it is easier to ask your butcher to prepare the pork for you. Ask him to remove the bones at the bottom and make a break in the bones along the side of the crown.

• Roast in a roasting dish. Fry onions until golden, add carrots, garlic then place crown on top and add water until half-covered. Add thyme, bay leaf and sage. Salt and pepper lightly and roast in a hot oven (200 to 210 °C) for 45 minutes to 1 hour depending on the size of the roast, turning occasionally. The addition of plenty of water ensures that the meat is not dry and, if the oven is not as hot, it will brown anyway.

• Meanwhile, lay slices of choriso on two baking trays and grill in a hot oven. They should be crisp and have lost all their fat.

As an accompaniment to the crown of pork, here is a recipe for mashed potatoes and olives.

Use potatoes of a variety recommended for mashing (150 g potatoes per person). Peel, cut into large cubes and cook, adding enough lightly salted water to cover potatoes but no more. When cooked, add single cream up to the halfway mark and continue cooking. The potatoes should be well cooked. They will almost be like a puree at this point. Finish mashing them with a fork and add 20 to 30 g of chopped black olives.

Lamb and aubergines

Serves 8

1.2 kg neck of lamb (boned but keep bones to make stock) • 8 large ripe tomatoes
6 large ripe aubergines • 2 courgettes • 1 whole garlic • 2 large onions
1 glass dry white wine • thyme, bay leaf • olive oil, salt, pepper

- Sauté neck of lamb. Use bones to make stock.
- At the same time, fry pieces of meat and add onions, garlic, thyme and bay leaf.
- Dice courgettes and tomatoes. Cook over a low heat for 2 hours with white wine.
- Thinly slice aubergine (lengthways), fry in olive oil then line small round moulds (for individual servings) or a gratin dish for a family meal.
- Place stew in the middle, cover with remainder of sliced aubergine.
- Complete cooking over a low heat for 30 minutes until tender.
- Serve with lamb gravy. Bind with few cloves garlic.

• Cut a boned leg of lamb into pieces approximately 90 g each in weight. Place a piece of diced bacon in each piece, taking care to insert along the direction of the fibres in the meat. The bacon should be seasoned with spiced salt.

• Marinate pieces of meat for 2 hours with 10 cl oil per litre of wine, chopped carrots and onions, four cloves garlic, thyme, bay leaf, and parsley stalks.

• Chop three onions and mix with two crushed cloves garlic. Blanch 250 g finely-diced gammon.

• Cut 250 g fresh bacon rind into 2 cm (almost 1 inch) squares. Blanch.

• Place dried orange peel in a bunch of parsley.

• Line base and sides of a terrine with thin strips of pork fat. Add pieces of lamb, alternating layers of meat with layers of onion, bacon and rind. Sprinkle thyme and powdered bay leaf over each layer.

• Place bunch of parsley in the middle of the terrine and season each layer lightly.

• Strain marinade through a Chinese sieve and pour over meat and vegetables. Seal the terrine and ensure that the steam is concentrated.

• Begin cooking on the hob then bake for 5 hours in a low oven, ensuring that the oven temperature does not vary during the cooking time.

• When ready to serve, take off lid, remove pork fat, remove any excess fat and take out the bunch of parsley.

• The stew is served as is, in the terrine.

Saddle of Rabbit
with liver stuffing

SERVES 2

1 SADDLE RABBIT • RABBIT'S LIVER • 1 WHOLE GARLIC • 200 G PRESERVED TOMATOES
SALT, PEPPER, THYME • CAUL • STOCK

- Bone saddle of rabbit, beginning by removing fillets. Remove bone without detaching flesh along back.
- Roughly dice liver, season with salt and pepper and dust with thyme.
- Place stuffing in centre of saddle. Roll in caul and tie up with string as if making a roast.
- Roast for 20 to 25 minutes in a very hot oven, with a whole garlic.
- Add 200 g preserved tomatoes at end of cooking time. Leave to rest.
- Deglaze with water or stock. Reduce down until clear and slightly "fatty".

Delicious served with a good red Gigondas.

Saddle of hare
with jugged gravy

Serves 2

1 saddle of hare • 4 cloves garlic • bay leaf, thyme, oil, balsamic vinegar
6 boiled potatoes to garnish

Jugged gravy: 1 kg game trimmings • 2 large onions • 1 stick celery • 3 cloves garlic
1 carrot • thyme, bay leaf • 2 litres côtes-du-rhône (made from syrah grapes)
or any other full-bodied wine • 2 cloves • 5 juniper berries • 80 g flour

- Fry game trimmings until brown.
- Fry onions and carrots until golden. Blend thyme, bay leaf, celery and garlic with trimmings. Add cloves and juniper berries and sprinkle on flour. Cook for a few minutes. Pour on wine.
- Simmer for 4 hours over a low heat.
- Strain gravy and reduce by half to produce a black, smooth gravy.
- Remove nerves from saddle of hare. Roast in a sauté pan. Brown on all sides. Add garlic, thyme and bay leaf.
- Finish cooking in a very hot oven (180-200 °C). This takes between 10 and 15 minutes. The meat should be pink. Remove from oven and leave to rest.
- Degrease sauté pan, add half a glass of balsamic vinegar. Reduce and add one quarter litre of jugged gravy. Cook over a very low heat for 5 to 6 minutes. Strain through a fine-meshed Chinese sieve, taking care to crush cloves of garlic.
- Correct seasoning. Reheat hare then remove bones. Serve in pieces, covered with gravy, and accompanied by boiled potatoes.

This dish is excellent with a good Gigondas.

Spelt and Sausage Soup

Serves 10

4 sausages • 300 g small spelt • 1 stick celery, thyme and bay leaf for a bouquet garni
1 carrot • 1 onion studded with 4 cloves

• Cook sausages in 3.5 litres water with vegetables and bouquet garni for 1 to 1 1/2 hours depending on size.

• Pour stock over spelt and cook for 30 to 40 minutes.

• Meanwhile, when sausages are cold, cut into thick slices (2 to 3 cm, approx. 1 in.) and grill. Add sliced sausages to soup as garnish.

This is a good, tasty winter soup which can be washed down with a glass of red wine (a Gigondas is a good choice).

Guinea Fowl with Olives

SERVES 8

1 GUINEA FOWL (1.8 TO 2 KG) • 200 G GREEN OLIVES (STONED) • 1 SHALLOT
1 LITRE STOCK • 1 LITRE DOUBLE CREAM • 25 CL WHITE WINE • OLIVE OIL, SALT, PEPPER

- Remove the fillets from the guinea fowl breasts.
- Make a fine stuffing (equal amounts of meat and cream).
- Pit and chop olives.
- Add olives to stuffing and season to taste.
- Open up breasts in half and add a spoonful of stuffing.
- Roll breasts in greaseproof paper. Poach in stock to cook.
- Sauté the boned thighs with cream and olives.
- Reduce stock to a glaze to make a concentrated liquor.

Guinea fowl with olives is fairly quick to prepare and it makes a delicious family meal if served with spelt or fresh pasta.

Roast Pigeon
with garlic

Serves 2

1 pigeon (600 to 650 g) • 6 cloves garlic • salt, pepper, rosemary, bay leaf

• Begin by flaming the pigeon. Many of my friends do not know what it means to flame a pigeon. In fact, it applies to a pigeon or any other poultry. Flaming means burning off the small feathers that remain on the legs, wings and breast. It should be done over a high flame. Quickly pass the poultry over the flame, turning it in all directions. All the small feathers will frizzle up.

• Then gut the pigeon. Cut off neck and legs and set aside to make gravy. Place a bay leaf and sprig of rosemary inside pigeon.

• Pot roast in a small pan scarcely bigger than the bird. Heat well then add neck and legs. Cook pigeon on one side (over a fairly strong heat) for 5 minutes then turn over and again cook for 5 minutes.

• Preheat oven to 180 to 200 °C. Put pigeon on its back, add cloves garlic and roast in the oven for 10 minutes.

• In Provence, pigeon is served slightly pink. If you prefer it well cooked, add 5 minutes to the roasting time.

• The pigeon should be golden brown when removed from oven. Leave to rest for 15 minutes to tenderise the meat.

• Degrease the saucepan and deglaze with a small glass water. Reduce down to a thick gravy.

Serve with thyme-flavoured potato cakes. This is a really mouthwatering dish.

Feet and Tripe Parcels

12 small lamb's tripe parcels • 6 lamb's feet • 1 pepper • 1 kg tomatoes
200 g carrots • 300 g onions • 1 litre white wine • olive oil

• Sweat vegetables with some olive oil. When golden brown, top with feet and tripe parcels. Add tomatoes last of all then season with salt and pepper and add pimento.

• Pour in 1 litre good white wine and bring up to the required level with water.

• Cook for 6 hours over a gentle heat. Once cooked, remove tripe parcels and feet.

• Recook sauce to remove any acidity.

Tripe parcels, known in the south of France as "paquets", are lamb's tripe stuffed with gammon, parsley and garlic, then cut into triangles, rolled up and tied with string. Personally, I recommend that you ask your tripe merchant to prepare them for you.

This dish is served piping hot with boiled potatoes.

Crown of Lamb
in sea salt

Serves 2

1 crown lamb (6 chops)

(ask your butcher to prepare the crown roast and give you the bones)

1 onion • 1 carrot • 3 cloves garlic • thyme, bay leaf

Salt crust: 500 g egg white (about 10 eggs)

1.5 kg sea salt • 500 g flour

- Lay bones on a baking tray. Preheat oven and roast bones till brown to make stock.
- To make the salt crust, mix together the sea salt, egg white and flour. Dress the crust around the lamb.
- Preheat oven to 240° C and bake for 20 minutes.
- Remove and rest for 15 to 20 minutes on a dish, turning occasionally to ensure that the blood circulates through the entire roast.
- Meanwhile, remove any fat on baking tray and fry onions, carrots and garlic. Pour on water to make sauce, add thyme and bay leaf and cook for a good half-hour. Strain through a fine Chinese sieve.
- Carve roast and moisten with gravy before serving. If crown roast has cooled, reheat before carving.

In Provence, lamb is the traditional choice for Easter Sunday. It should not be too fatty nor too pink. It should be almost white and very slightly veined.

STAUB

Vegetables

Ratatouille

Serves 10

2 kg tomatoes • 600 g aubergines • 100 g courgettes • 4 large onions
4 green peppers • 6 cloves garlic • thyme, bay leaf, olive oil, salt, pepper

• Finely dice all vegetables, beginning with peppers. Blanch for a few minutes in a good quantity of water (this makes them more digestible).

• Chop aubergines and courgettes, making sure that pieces are all the same size then sauté in a hot pan with olive oil. They should be allowed to colour slightly. Drain in a colander because the vegetables absorb a lot of oil (especially the aubergines). Keep oil to make vinaigrettes with. They will be full of flavour and aroma.

• Meanwhile, skin tomatoes, remove pips, then chop roughly with a large knife.

• Chop onions and sweat in a large pan until almost transparent. Add tomatoes and cook until liquor has almost reduced away. Add garlic, thyme, bay leaf, salt and pepper.

• Mix in all the vegetables: courgettes, aubergines, tomatoes and peppers. Boil for a few minutes.

Ratatouille is the all-time great Provençal dish and there is always some in the refrigerator during the summer. It can be eaten cold or hot and the vegetables can be cut in several different ways. Purists will tell you that they must be roughly diced; these days, chefs tend to dice the vegetables finely and avoid overcooking them. This method gives the vegetables more flavour and, more importantly, ensures that they retain their beautiful colours.

Fennel can add a touch of freshness and a hint of aniseed. This is an excellent, fresh recipe which goes well with a Rosé de Tavel, Domaine du Vieux-Relais.

Cream of Lentil Soup

Serves 10

300 g green lentils • 1 carrot • 1 onion • 2 cloves garlic • 100 g salt pork (roughly diced) • 2.5 litres water • 25 cl whipped cream • olive oil

• Sweat diced pork in olive oil. Once it is golden brown, add lentils, pour over water and add vegetables. Cook for a good hour, remove vegetables and mash. Check and correct seasoning. Add a few drops of olive oil.

• Just before serving, add whipped cream and blend well in a liquidiser.

In Provence, lentils were traditionally cooked with a piece of salt pork in a large quantity of water. The cooking liquor was served as a clear soup with dry bread and the lentils were eaten either as a salad or warm with the salt pork. With a main course to follow, there was enough for the week.

This soup can also be eaten cold. It has a very subtle taste and, with the addition of well-flavoured olive oil, it is absolutely delicious.

Pistou Soup

100 g large green beans • 100 g white haricot beans • 2 or 3 courgettes
100 g carrots • 50 g potatoes • 100 g large vermicelli
4 very ripe tomatoes • 5 cloves garlic • 1 bunch basil • 75 g parmesan cheese
25 cl olive oil • 2.5 litres water

• Top, tail and string green beans and cut into pieces. Dice courgettes.

• Cook green beans in 2.5 litres water with salt and pepper. After 15 minutes, add carrots and potatoes. After a further 15 minutes add courgettes.

• Cook for 15 minutes then add vermicelli.

• Crush tomato flesh, peeled garlic, parmesan and basil leaves, gradually dribbling on olive oil.

• Pour into boiling soup.

This soup originated in Genoa. It is now served piping hot in the autumn and cold in the summer. It can be made more or less refreshing depending on the quantity of tomatoes used.

Preserved Turnip
in balsamic vinegar

Serves 6

12 small white turnips • 25 cl balsamic vinegar • salt, pepper • 2 tbsp olive oil

- Peel turnips. N.B. in winter they have two skins, so peel thickly.
- Cut into rounds and blanch well in lightly salted water.
- In a large pan, reduce the vinegar by half. Add turnips and cook until vinegar has fully evaporated. The turnips will turn black.
- Add some pepper and olive oil – et voilà!
- This is an unusual but mouthwatering vegetable dish.

Turnips no longer enjoy the place they once had in recipe books. They are delicious served with red meats or grilled fish.

Cream of Celery Soup

SERVES 6

1 KG LEEKS (WHITE PARTS ONLY) • 1 KG CELERIAC • 50 CL VEAL STOCK
SLICED BREAD • BUTTER, OLIVE OIL • SALT, PEPPER

• Finely chop white parts of leeks and sweat slowly in olive oil in a saucepan.

• Finely dice celeriac, add to leeks and pour on 1/2 litre of veal stock and an equal quantity of water.

• Leave soup to cook. Meanwhile, fry tiny croutons of bread in butter. The croutons give the soup a "bit of bite".

• When the celeriac is cooked, blend as for a vegetable soup preferably in a Moulinette (a liquidiser puts too much air into the vegetables and changes the taste).

• Check seasoning and pour over small croutons.

The celeriac should soften the hearts of your guests!

Early Vegetables
in Poulette sauce

Serves 6

1 kg peas • 1 kg mange-tout peas • 1 kg purple artichokes
2 kg asparagus (or 1 kg asparagus tips) • 1 kg young carrots • 1 head celery
1 litre stock • 3 egg yolks • 50 cl cream • 100 g butter
1 lemon (juice only) • fines herbes

• Wash and peel vegetables. Shape artichoke hearts and cut into quarters. Cut celery and carrots into pieces of approximately the same size to improve the appearance of the dish. Cook separately in salted water and cool immediately by plunging into iced water.

• Make Poulette Sauce. Bring stock to boil and reduce by half. Blend in cream. Bring back to boil and pour over egg yolks, whisking as if making custard.

• Return to a gentle heat, being careful not to boil, and stir continuously. Gradually mix in butter. Add lemon juice and fines herbes.

• Reheat vegetables slightly and mix everything together.

Lay out on a serving dish. This is an excellent hors d'oeuvre with a white Châteauneuf-du-Pape wine.

Stewed Mange-tout Peas
with bacon

1 kg mange-tout peas • 100 g fresh, diced bacon • 2 onions • 4 cloves garlic
50 cl beef stock • 5 cl olive oil • 50 g preserved tomatoes • salt, pepper

• Fry bacon and chopped onions in olive oil. Add garlic and mange-tout peas with 50 cl beef stock and simmer over a low heat for 10 minutes. Season with salt and pepper.

• Lay out in a round and pour beef stock and arrange preserved tomatoes on the outside.

Red or Green Peppers
with olive oil

Serves 4

4 red peppers • 4 green peppers • 2 cloves garlic

• Take red and green peppers, cut in half, remove seeds and place, open side uppermost, on a baking tray. Season with salt and pepper, sprinkle with oil, and place in a very hot oven (200 to 210 °C) until the skins crack and become almost black.

• Remove from oven and cover with a teatowel. They are then very easy to peel.

• Place in a terrine and cover with oil, a small quantity of garlic and a few sprigs of thyme.

In summer, when peppers are in season, they are wonderful with olive oil. They can be served with an aperitif or as a garnish for patés and salads.

They can be served at any time, with toast made from a farmhouse loaf.

Round Nice Courgettes
stuffed with marjoram

Serves 6

6 round courgettes (80 to 100 g) • 1 onion (chopped) • 2 cloves garlic (chopped) • 30 g marjoram • 2 egg yolks • 2 tbsp double cream • olive oil

• Cut courgettes one-third down from the stalk end. Spoon out interior (taking care not to perforate the skin). Blanch in salted water, with their "hats".

• Meanwhile, sweat onion in a small quantity of olive oil. When onion is transparent, add courgette flesh and garlic and simmer until liquor has reduced away. Stir frequently to form a sort of puree. Add cream.

• Reduce further, almost by half. Cool. Mix in egg yolks, and check seasoning. Add chopped marjoram.

• Dry courgettes well with a teatowel or kitchen paper. Fill with stuffing and replace "hats". Bake in an oven at 160 °C. Pour on some olive oil and cook for 2 to 2 1/2 hours. The stuffing is cooked when it resembles an egg custard.

The courgettes can be eaten hot with a herb vinaigrette or cold. They are also delicious with large cuts of meat such as a rib of beef.

People in Northern France only discovered them some fifty years ago. Because of this, they tend to peel them; in the South of France they are eaten with their skin.

White-beet
au gratin

Serves 10

1 kg white-beet • 180 g grated parmesan • 1 litre bechamel sauce
(100 g butter, 80 g flour, 1 litre milk, salt, pepper, nutmeg)

• Separate green leaves from stems. Wash green leaves well and cook for 10 minutes in salted water. Quickly cool in iced water. Drain and set aside.

• Peel stems, removing as many strings as possible. Cut into pieces 10 cm (4 inches) long and 0.5 cm (1/4 inch) wide. Cook in salted water for 15 to 20 minutes. Cool, drain and set aside.

• Make bechamel sauce: melt butter then add flour and stir slowly with a wooden spoon. Bring milk to boil and gradually whisk into butter/flour roux. The sauce should be smooth and free from lumps. If lumps do form, strain through a Chinese sieve or liquidise. Cook for a few minutes.

• Meanwhile, finely chop green part of white-beet. Mix with stems and lay out in a gratin dish. Pour over bechamel sauce and sprinkle with grated parmesan. Bake in the oven until well browned (hot oven: 160 to 170°C).

This dish is an ideal accompaniment to roast meats, loin of veal or leg of lamb. I recommend a light red wine from Cairanne or Lirac.

Cream of Marrow

Serves 10

3 kg marrow • 2 leaks (white parts only) • 3 cloves garlic • 80 g butter
1 litre single cream • 50 cl milk • salt, pepper, olive oil, nutmeg

• Peel and roughly dice marrow. Finely chop white parts of leeks and sweat in butter in a large sauté pan. Leave to blanch.

• Add diced marrow and garlic cloves. Stir on low heat for 20 to 25 minutes then add milk and single cream. Leave to simmer, stirring continually.

• The marrow should soften in the sauté pan and become smooth. Strain then season with salt and pepper and a little nutmeg.

• Add a few drops of olive oil for flavour.

You may also add 50 g chopped truffles at the last moment when the cream is piping hot.

Stuffed Artichokes

Serves 4

12 purple artichokes • 2 carrots • 2 onions • 1 whole garlic
1 stick celery • 1 bunch basil • olive oil, thyme, bay leaf • stock

- Shape artichokes and retain white leaves.
- Dice carrots, onions and celery.
- Finely chop white artichoke leaves and stew gently with remainder of the vegetables.
- Fill artichoke hearts. Braise in stock with roughly chopped garlic, thyme and bay leaf.
- Simmer for 20 to 30 minutes depending on size. Remove hearts from pan.
- Reduce stock. Add chopped basil and check seasoning.

Tomatoes
à la Provençale

Serves 4

8 large, ripe tomatoes • 50 g garlic • 1 sprig flat parsley
150 g white breadcrumbs • salt, pepper • olive oil • thyme

• Preheat the oven.

• Chop garlic and parsley.

• Cut tomatoes in half. Press them sharply to remove seeds.

• Lay tomatoes out on a baking tray or in a gratin dish.

• Season with salt and pepper and dust with thyme.

• Mix parsley and garlic with a little olive oil and the breadcrumbs to form a thick, fatty paste.

• Fill tomatoes with paste and cook for 20 to 30 minutes at 150 to 160 °C.

There are umpteen thousand recipes for tomatoes à la provençale. Every mother and grandmother has her own. Every family and every household has its own. And everybody swears that theirs is the only authentic recipe and the best. Of course, everybody claims to be right!

Braised Fennel
with saffron

Serves 6

6 fennel heads • 2 onions • thyme, bay leaf • 1 carrot • 2 cloves garlic
25 cl white wine • 1 g saffron • salt, pepper • olive oil

• Cut heads in half. Remove hard leaves (they can be used to make a cream or a soup). Blanch well in salted water and leave to cool.

• Meanwhile, finely dice onions and carrot (3 mm pieces). Crush garlic and sauté with onions and carrot in a small quantity of olive oil. The sauté pan should be large enough to take all the ingredients.

• When onions and carrots have sweated well, lay fennel on top. Ensure that none of the pieces is touching. Add thyme and bay leaf. Mix saffron into white wine and pour into sauté pan. Add water to cover vegetables. Bring to boil, season with salt and pepper.

• Cover and simmer gently in the oven (180 °C) for 2 hours.

• When cooked, remove fennel. Reduce sauce then strain through a Chinese sieve and add some olive oil to emulsify.

This is wonderful with grilled fish or white meats.

Tomato, Aubergine and Mozzarella Slice

Serves 6

8 tomatoes • 4 aubergines • 200 g mozzarella • garlic, shallot thyme, bay leaf • 50 cl olive oil • pepper

• Slice aubergines into rounds and cook in olive oil until deep golden on both sides. Cut tomatoes into rounds and fry over a high heat. At the last moment, add chopped garlic and shallot, a few sprigs of thyme and powdered bay leaf.

• Put alternating layers of aubergine and tomatoes in moulds. Bake in a hot oven (150 °C) for 30 minutes.

• Moisten sauce slightly with olive oil. Add mozzarella cheese in between the aubergine and tomato rounds.

• Dribble with liquor.

This dish can be eaten on its own, as a hot hors d'oeuvre or even cold, with a vinaigrette. A good rosé or a light red are excellent as an accompaniment.

Desserts

Citrus Rectangles

1 kg flour • 40 g sugar • 3 oranges (grated) • 2 lemons (grated) • 10 g ground nut oil
1/2 orange (juice only) • 125 g melted sugar • 3 eggs • icing sugar

• Knead flour, sugar, eggs, orange juice, lemon and orange zests to obtain a smooth paste.

• Mix in melted butter.

• Roll out fairly thinly. Cut out rectangles and fry in very hot oil then drain on kitchen paper.

• Once cooked and drained, dust with icing sugar.

Lemon and Basil Sorbet

1.25 LITRES WATER • 450 G SUGAR • 300 G LEMON JUICE • 1/2 BUNCH BASIL

• Mix water, sugar, lemon juice and basil.

• Bring to boil then strain through a fine-meshed Chinese sieve. Put in deep freeze and as soon as it begins to “take”, scrape with a fork.

This is a simple recipe and it is very refreshing in hot weather.

Honey-braised Peaches
with lavender ice cream

Serves 4

600 g peaches (quartered) • 1 tbsp lavender honey

Ice cream: 50 cl milk • 6 egg yolks • 125 g sugar • natural lavender flavouring (quantity is a matter of personal choice)

- Make lavender ice cream.
- Braise peaches in a frying pan with butter and honey.
- Lay peach quarters round edge of plate.
- Pour warm honey remaining in frying pan over peaches.
- Place a scoop of lavender ice cream in the centre of the plate.

Quince Turnovers

Serves 4

4 ripe quince • puff pastry • 4 tbsp apple compote • 1 egg yolk

Syrup: 1 litre water • 750 g sugar

• Make syrup with 1 litre water and sugar. Cook whole quince, with skin, in syrup. Leave in syrup to cool.

• Meanwhile, prepare 4 rounds of pastry 20 cm (8 inches) in diameter and 3 mm thick.

• Dice quince, removing pips but leaving skin.

• Spread compote in middle of pastry and top with diced quince.

• Fold pastry to make turnover and seal with egg yolk.

• Use remaining egg yolk to brush over pastry.

• Prick with fork and bake in an oven preheated to 180 °C.

• Bake for 20 minutes.

I advise you to eat them while warm. They are tastier hot than cold.

Lavender-flavoured Creme brûlée

SERVES 4 TO 6

6 EGG YOLKS • 100 G CASTER SUGAR • 250 G SINGLE CREAM
10 CL MILK • 1 G DRIED LAVENDER

- Mix egg yolks with sugar, whisking swiftly until white.
- Add cream, cold milk and lavender.
- Leave mixture to rest for 1 or 2 hours to pick up full flavour of the lavender.
- Pour into an egg dish or ovenproof pottery plate.
- Bake at 130 °C in a bain-marie for 1 1/4 hours.
- Remove from oven and allow to cool.

It is advisable to make this dish in the morning for the evening meal.

Caramelised Apples

Serves 6

1 kg apples (golden delicious or cox's) • 1 bottle cider
1/2 glass apple brandy ("calvados") • 200 g sugar • 200 g honey • 100 g butter

• Peel apples and cut into eight. Remove pips.

• Make caramel with butter, honey and sugar. As soon as caramel begins to turn brown, add apples and sauté.

• When apples are well coated with caramel, cook gently for 3 to 4 minutes.

• Remove from pan and lay on a serving dish.

• Deglaze remaining caramel with apple brandy, after removing pan from heat. The sauce should be a warm golden colour. Drizzle round the apples.

Fennel Sorbet

900 g caster sugar • 12 g stabiliser • 300 g dried fennel • 2 litres water

- Place sugar, stabiliser and dried fennel in a saucepan.
- Pour on 1 litre water and bring to boil.
- When mixture begins to boil, turn off heat and leave to infuse for approximately 30 minutes. Then add second litre of water.
- Leave until cold and mix.

Pine-kernel Tart

Serves 8

Pastry: 125 g butter • 125 g sugar • 4 egg yolks
250 g flour • salt • 1 vanilla pod
Filling: 100 g sugar • 100 g butter
400 g pine-kernels • 25 cl double cream

• Mix butter, sugar and pinch of salt and beat until smooth and white.

• Gradually add egg yolks. Blend in flour. Beat as little as possible. Leave for 4 hours before using.

• Roll out pastry and line a sufficiently large tin for 8 people. Bake blind for a few minutes in a hot oven (200 °C).

• Make a pale caramel with butter. Add pine-kernels.

• Cook then deglaze with cream.

• Put back over heat for a few minutes with cream.

• Pour pine-kernel and cream mixture into pastry case.

• Bake for 20 minutes at 160 °C.

Darphin Apples

Ingredients for 1 person

1 apple • 2 eggs • caster sugar • few drops lemon juice
3 cl cognac

• Peel and grate apple. Sprinkle with sugar while grating and, if necessary, add few drops of lemon juice to prevent apple from discolouring. Add cognac and mix well.

• Beat eggs and blend into apple mixture. Cook like an omelette with a small knob of butter. Turn omelette over and cook other side.

Provençal Shuttles

750 g flour • 375 g caster sugar • 65 g butter • 3 eggs
10 cl water • 1 lemon (zest only) • salt

• Make a fountain with flour and place sugar, softened butter, zests, a pinch of salt, and eggs in centre. Blend in water to obtain a smooth paste.

• Make sausage shapes of the size preferred. Cut into sections and pat into an oval shape.

• Lay on a greased baking sheet. Slash centre of each shuttle and leave for 1 hour. Brush with egg yolk.

• Bake at a moderate temperature and remove from oven when shuttles are golden brown.

Quince Jujube

- Select ripe quince. Wash and quarter, with skin and pips.
- Place in a saucepan, barely cover with water and cook.
- When soft, drain and strain through a Moulinette.
- Weigh the puree and use 1 kg sugar to 1 kg puree.
- Place in a preserving pan and cook gently, stirring all the time.
- Ask somebody to help you with this recipe. It takes at least half-an-hour and your arm will tire quickly as you move the wooden spoon continuously back and forward through the mixture.
- To test whether the quince jujube is cooked, pour a small quantity onto a plate. If it remains compact, it is ready. Pour mixture onto a baking tray and leave to cool.
- Cut into pieces to suit requirements.

Pompe à huile
or fougasse

125 g and 325 g flour • 150 g sugar • 10 cl olive oil • 1 orange
1 lemon • 20 g baker's yeast • 1 egg yolk
2 tbsp orange flower water

- On previous day, prepare a leaven with 125 g flour, baker's yeast and 8 cl water.
- Leave to rise overnight.
- The next day, grate zests of orange and lemon. Place 325 g flour in a mixing bowl and make a well in the centre. Add sugar, salt, oil and orange flower water. Mix with leaven to obtain a smooth dough. Leave to rise for 30 minutes.
- Beat dough on the work surface to remove all fermenting gases.
- Roll out to 1 cm (1/2 inch) thick. Cut out rectangles and slash in middle with a knife.
- Bake in an oven preheated to 180 °C for 20 minutes.

This is the Provençal recipe par excellence. It is a vital part of traditional Christmas celebrations.

White Nougat

700 g honey • 175 g egg whites, heated and beaten until stiff • 400 g glucose
800 g sugar • 30 cl water • 900 g whole roasted almonds

- Pour cooked sugar (glucose + sugar + water cooked at 140 °C) and honey over stiffly-beaten egg whites. Leave until cold.
- Add hot almonds. Pour immediately onto a well-greased baking tray and leave until cold.
- Cut pieces of the required size.

Recipe Index

Hors d'œuvres

Fish

Meat dishes

Vegetables

Desserts

Restaurant Christian Etienne - 10, rue de Mons - 84000 Avignon, France

Éditions Ouest-France would like to thank Catherine Auguste
for her permission to use patterns from
Motifs provençaux à connaître et à créer published by Éditions Ouest-France.

Photo credits

The photo report of these recipes was made by Didier Benaouda.

P10: © RIEGER Bertrand / hemis.fr
P34: © BARBIER Bruno / hemis.fr
P60: © CAVALIER Michel / hemis.fr
P112: © MOIRENC Camille / hemis.fr

Editor: Marilyn Zermatten – Editorial coordination: Aline Ngo-Doan-Ta
Graphic design and layout: Editions Ouest-France graphic studio
Photoengraving: graph&ti (35) - Printing: Pollina, Luçon (85) - L59024
Publisher no.: 6773.01.02.01.12 - I.S.B.N. 978-2-7373- 5669-8
Legal deposit January 2012
Printed in France

www.editionsouestfrance.fr